# Lauren at Two

# Lauren at Two

❧

Serge Lecomte

LAUREN AT 20

# Acknowledgments

The following poems appeared in Mildred (1991):
"The sound barrier," "Space voyager,"
"My little helper," "Harvesting," "Halloween night,"
"They're forecasting snow," and "Our walks."

# LAUREN LECOMTE (1989–2009)

L AUREN LECOMTE WAS BORN on January 25, 1989 in Fairbanks. The moment Lauren stepped onto this planet I was certain she was from another galaxy. She almost immediately took off on her own two feet to discover the world around her. Everything interested her. She smelled almost everything she touched and petted all the animals she knew. The moment she came out of her mother's belly, she heard the written word read to her. She became one of the most avid readers I have ever seen. She loved books. Eventually, she wrote some of her own stories. Her English was impeccable and she could speak it a mile a minute. She had so much to say about everything, but she didn't share her thoughts with everyone, only the select few.

Lauren became an independent thinker early on and she went out into the world without fear. She was accepting of all human beings and even extraterrestrials. She never had a bad word to say about people of different backgrounds or color. She could step into the New York subway and talk to the first stranger she met. Where I sometimes saw danger, my daughter saw opportunities to hear other people. Yet, she didn't make close friends easily in high school, as she was insecure about herself. But when she arrived at the university, she made friends. She wanted to be accepted for who she was, and she needed to be heard. Above all, she wanted to be loved, as most of us do, and she returned that love in kind. Yet, she learned to love those she didn't know and helped them out. She had the kindest heart in the world.

Lauren traveled this globe with me several times. When she was two she sold poetry books door to door and was taken to the police station with her dad for soliciting. When she was five she traveled to New York to see her grandmother and to see the musical *Cats*, and saw several polar bears and penguins at the Central Park Zoo. In 2003, she drove across Canada and then flew to New York City. In 2007 she went to the Carnival of Binche in Belgium to see her dad's relatives for the first time.

She had a wild time, dancing. She also learned to salsa and rumba. She had feet that moved to many different drums. She loved life with all her passion.

Lauren was very human and there was something sad in her smile that seemed to light up the room. She had many conflicts with herself, the world and some people, but in spite of that she loved us all. Lauren was born with a special gift: she couldn't hold a grudge. She was able to step out of herself and analyze a particular situation and explain why she couldn't get along with a person. She especially had a lot of love and compassion for her mother. She loved her brother Nikos, her bosom buddy the day he was born. He misses her a lot as we all do. She graduated from Lathrop High School in 2007 and subsequently attended the University of Alaska in Fairbanks where she died of bulimia on February 3rd, 2009.

Lauren still had a lot of things to do. She was planning to get her Doctorate in Psychology. She was going to get her driver's license this February. She wanted to either work as a deckhand in Homer or go to summer school. She also wanted to visit her sister Melissa in Atlanta and see her nephews Isaac and Ethan. She would have loved her niece Adeleide. Lauren's plate was always full. She will have to pass these inconsequential things up on this trip. I actually think she has bigger fish to fry. Once she heard there was a seat on the last spaceship out, she opted off this planet to see what a better part of the universe looked like. Lauren was just passing through earth to say hi and to tell us how much she loved us all.

# *Fishing*

The technician is fishing
for the tadpole that will be you
to catch what the eye can't see
through your mother's belly.
He sounds the water's depth
and zeroes in on your flesh
floating on a lifeline
like a tiny toy astronaut
secure in its womb – a universe
from which you will emerge
like the salmon dying upstream
after a long swim home.

You are a girl before your birth,
name already tagged on to you,
like an opened present
gutted before the appointed hour of celebration.

One of my friends hates the five daughters he begat,
wishing for a son every time he came into his wife
for a piece of immortality.
His wife's pregnant again
and he's got his harpoon ready for the seal hunt
as the sonar locates another daughter,
he will pluck out of the ice hole
and throw its bloody body back into the ocean
until he's found one with the right features.

# *Resurrection*

The water has broken at the entrance of the cave
where I knelt like a pilgrim yearning for wonder.
I called you Fletus the Fetus,
speaking to you in Spanish and Chinese,
wishing you smooth sailing in future travels.

I played Mozart on your Mother's belly
to the approval of the dancer
she hopes you'll become,
should my language lessons fail your tongue
still too confused to pronounce caca.
I pray you'll not confuse me with poop
and dance the minuet instead.

It is time for you to eject
like a seed out of its shell
and take root near your Mother's breast
bleeding milk as if blood from a wound
that will heal you both with a smile.

Your head squeezes out like a sponge,
triangular, black as a kitten,
through my tears that hold death at bay.

# *Your playground*

Your hand reaches for the fire
like a moth oblivious to pain,
but you shriek as though abused by some criminal parent
as I pull you away from obvious danger.
An un-acrobatic clown you stumble with certainty
for lack of a net below
raising our expectations
as you climb to the window with prints now unfamiliar
your Mt. Olympus or Fuji —
to stare at your newly acquired features
in the reflection that still puzzles you.

In search of self,
you unload drawers of spoons, forks, knives,
bread pans, wooden bowls and a box of cornflakes.
You empty my shelves of books
whose pages your censor out of frustration.
You manage to climb a chair
under my all-seeing eyes;
then strain to touch the bowl and last apple
that stands as a reminder of future failures
yet undefined by your tiny hand
testing the limits of its will
as it slaps mine away,
wanting no guidance from above.

# The sound barrier

I follow in my daughter's footsteps,
imprinting like a gander with a distant recollection
of the egg it hatched out of.
The rain and mud make no difference to her.
It's just like the jelly and fruit
she blesses our guests with on Sundays.

They won't be back, they said,
until she's outgrown her wild stage,
a phase Bartholomew relinquished months ago.
He is obedient but speaks when asked.
He can even count to a hundred.
Bartholomew and my daughter are the same age.

I follow in the footsteps of the wild daughter
I have engendered, not without passion.
Her mouth is as mute as the flight of cranes
zigzagging south under the illusion of eternal summers.

With her there are no words for pebbles,
leaves, mud; all end up in the same pail,
where nature has no biology
and clouds metamorphose into ever-changing creatures
that make her laugh as I have forgotten to laugh.

The silence from her lips bathes us both
as I follow like a Buddhist monk
in search of the true Warrior within.
My wife fears our daughter might never speak.
What a horrifying thought, she said,

she will never know the songs that life can offer!
The doctor warned
that once she breaks the sound barrier
there is no going back.

# *The dragon*

The Berlin Wall has been sold;
others have been found, to hate.
And that's okay, for the sake of peace.
My two-year-old daughter knows better,
staring at the hairy gorilla soaking in the tub.
The pipes will freeze if I close the door.
Nakedness doesn't bother me
as it disturbs those into clothes, hair and make-up,
those into hatred of fat, Blacks...
anyone not reflected in the vanity mirror.
My teeth chatter from the lack of warmth.
The water is frozen on the river.
Death has been declared illegal by Congress,
except for those of a different persuasion.
Democracy means Coca-Cola for all
with the illusion of individual liberties.
Pepsi is for Red Russians and Chinese.

My daughter rubs soap on my back...
I feel old today
as she comforts the naked fetus I have become.
A student threatened to blow my brains out
for the B that killed his 4.0 GPA.
A's are in style, like sacred icons.
Our secretary thinks I'm a spy
because I teach Arabic.
Arabs are sinful, she says,
'cause they don't believe in our Lord Jesus Christ.
They won't go to Heaven, she continues,
'cause they have all the oil,

and Christians always share
even what they don't have.
Her brother's in Saudi Arabia
and Catholic to the core.

I dissolve nerves and muscles back to jelly
to retrieve the man I left at home this morning
and flush the dirt and thoughts back out
where they belong.
My wife steps lightly,
careful not to disturb the dragon in his lair
composing tomorrow's lessons;
only my daughter dares enter
to put out the fire that might burn down the house
should I breathe too passionately.

# *Our walks*

We will not let the zero weather deter us from our walks,
you and I tied to metal and cloth
that hold you up in the air
dependent of my back
like a modern-day papoose.
A marsupial with its pouch on backwards
I wish I had your mother's breasts
to allay your fears of the night forests,
to comfort myself.

We walk,
I naming the Pileated Woodpecker against an early snow,
left-over birch leaves,
a moose and calf sauntering across the road
in search of broccoli stems and willow,
the taste of summer too quickly deadened.
A squirrel hangs above our heads
like an acrobat with a pine cone for an umbrella.
It squeaks like the piggy we bought you.
You giggle, perhaps amazed by the similarity.
We walk,
in search of skies without antennas.
Our neighbors are trying to keep in touch with the universe,
receiving shows from as far as Japan.
We do not enter their domains anymore.
You see, my daughter,
you tried to hug men and women on one of their sets,
thinking we were them.

We walk...
Beware, my dear, that's an antenna, not a bird.
Pretty soon people will wear them on their heads
to facilitate reception.

# *When do I tell you about God?*

Shall I tell you of the God
that used to fly out of my father's oily mouth
as a bird with a lizard tail
and the head of a goat
to visit my bed in the dark
where I prayed, eyes shut,
for the forgiveness of guilt
instilled for sins
defined by a man who breathed coal dust all his life
and felt the whip unleashed by his own father's fears?

Shall I frighten you the child into obedience
and drag you into the pits of hell
where He sits,
head crowned with horns of gold and rubies,
lopping off children's heads,
as fragile as poppies,
for telling lies because of love denied?

Shall I tell you of the Christmases
that saw no trees in our living room?
Or of the Christ dead in the manger
before He had a chance to suffer the crucifixion
because His father loved lamb?

The earth you stand on is a Goddess
you must love to love.
She is everything you touch, smell and taste
what God cannot.
His sinuses are numb,
and it is written
that He had no, has no, and will never have any taste buds!
God isn't really God,

and it sure ain't Santa
even if the other kids tell you so.
Every child is a Jesus at birth
until Santa gets a hold of her
and exchanges toys for her soul.
Underneath that jolly old bowl full of jelly
there is a dirty old man.

As you touch, kill and create the universe you choose,
you too are a goddess
as long as you remain ignorant of the Word
that could lead you astray.

# *My magician*

Just when I think I'm going blind
(wishfully thinking so)
although there is nothing clinically wrong
with my carrot-eating eyes,
my daughter pokes me in the pupils
to make sure
they're not the blueberries
she grazed on last week,
her mouth still blue
and smiling
in spite of the pain inflicted.

Just when I hope to lose my hearing
and find Buddhist bliss
in some dark uncharted forest,
my daughter drags me out of bed
with shredding shrills
that would restore life
to those dead not wishing to relive reruns.
She then makes me sing forgotten songs
to appease dream-slaughtering beasts
and allows me to fly with moths
to the other side of the moon
to see if the cow really jumped over;
there I can shed clothes and skin
and be a gecko clicking on a ceiling
looking to have a better view.

# Fearless Lauren

There was the day
you ate a bear's nose
until it couldn't breathe
and it escaped roaring into a primeval forest.

There was the night
your toothless mouth refused the breast
and it chose to swallow the rising sun
on a shirt made in Japan.

All that's history,
already forgotten,
because it was long ago – a year.

Now that you've turned the house upside down,
you are ready to map the world outside these walls,
like an aimless navigator,
unsure of the uncharted sea.

Like a sail, you venture out of port
in your red raincoat
(to better to see you, my dear).
The wind gives you the confidence
to balance your unsteady gait
as you climb down the driveway
under your mother's magnifying eye
like a hawk perched on the windowsill.

Your search leads to pebbles and golden leaves,
hands busy to touch the unknown.
Undaunted, you pick dandelions and raspberries,
your mouth and nose attuned to their taste.

You're doing fine, your mother says proudly,
until you scream bloody murder
under attack from hornets in the shed
that manage to sting your ear and forehead.

I run out to soothe your pain
and whisper that this garden is also full of snakes
even if there are none indigenous to our land.

# Dog in the manger

You baptized them Mary, Nelly and Billy,
blessed them with a kiss
and carefully buried them in boxes forgotten,
to play with the newness of catalogues you tore
to see if things are truly worth a thousand words.
They weren't.
So you abandoned maimed bears, legless dolls,
like a miniature warrior
unaware that girls can do if allowed to do
what boys now do with the Hallowed ground.
You were bored.
Some would say you wanted to go exploring,
but they don't know you
as well as I could know the person you will be,
like me.

There is a knock at the door,
and the fish you are dipping for are spared
as I prevent you from falling into an ocean
I forgot to explore when I was you.
One of your small friends stands on the threshold,
come to play with his favorites.
Unaware of you, he rushes for Mary, Nelly and Billy
and resurrects them with a crushing hug
smiling at the comfort he is giving himself,
his mother driving off to Psychology 101.
Stunned by his brashness,
you attempt to wrestle the babies you deserted
after killing them last night
because you couldn't climb the stairs
to heights that open to shelves prohibited.

I mediate with common sense
emotions cannot comprehend,
feeling like Mr. Spock, inhuman and unpopular,
with both of you screaming to possess
what things belong to others
wanting all three – Mary, Nelly and Billy –
or none.

# They're forecasting snow

The raven has swallowed the sun
to keep its belly warm.

You slither into our bed
to poison your mother's dreams
in search of the breast
like a leech seeking comfort
from the dark that once enveloped you.
Today isn't a good day!
Your mother feels sorry for you though
as you kick me in the ribs, groin...
until I am exiled by your presence
from the garden I thought mine
until you were born
as if by God's design
catalogue ordered.

I lie like a dog near the stove,
thoughts floating up the flue:
the IRS has threatened to take our house,
my colleagues keep studying slugs,
my father's breathing pure oxygen
somewhere in Los Angeles,
hoping death will claw him out
of the soaps he's drowning in
to free himself from his own lungs.

You cry out no particular name
to see which of us you can soften.
Like a jack in a box I spring up the stairs.
This is just the beginning...

They're forecasting snow.

# *You want my heart*

Carrion
I perch
at the edge of my desk,
expecting them
to pick my brains
to gain knowledge without pain.
A pill would suffice
to feed
their wanting.
They want
to share my tongue
to speak with eloquence
the Chinese it took me years
on the island with the natives.

The phone rings again.
They want
all ears to hear
their pleas, excuses, lies,
pains and loneliness,
never laughter
or love.
Love would be as indecent as aggravated assault
or picking God's forbidden fruit
or nose for that matter.
I would make a lousy confessor.
Maybe that's why I forsook the Church.

They find the above irreverent.
They write down objectionable words:
semen, transvestites, kisses, and kin
into unrecyclable waste.
They believe in God – a linguistic purist –

incapable of saying or writing anything
obscene.
God never made records or cassettes, I tell them.
They are ready
to crucify.

I am but a skeleton driving home.
The couch is my coffin
where I sleep with my solitude,
depression dreaming of snares
it sets in lakes still unfrozen in my brain.
But you will not allow them
to catch the fish that get away.
You are only two,
and you only want
my heart
wounded but beating still.

# *You want to pet*

You've now petted away
your fear of tigers
in the cat next door
that pleaded for its life
with you laughing
wild forest cries
as its claws wrenched
the feline out of you
strangling phobia
into tears,
you unable to kill the hunt.
That was yesterday.

Today you're pounding at your image,
trying to break the Ice Palace
ready to conquer the canine world
with one bite of my thigh!
Perhaps if you think yourself a dog,
they will understand,
but it's a dog eat dog world out there,
I forgot.
I could tell you of the dogs          .
that carried off chunks of my brother
the mailman
and of his subsequent vengeance
with his Colt .45
taking dogs and Puerto Ricans down
and of his subsequent hospitalization
because of death
haunting his dreams
since the war.

I could tell you of dogs
taught to eat children for dessert
and of dogs
vegetarians feed horsemeat religiously,
and you would weep for the colt your rode
and curse the dog God made
in rabid anger
to protect his Garden from the snake,
and I would understand
your love for snakes
because you are a girl.
Yet you still want to pet the illusion
of pups and stuffed toys,
not knowing when bites are worse that the bark.

# *Insulation*

A dog,
breed and owner unknown,
pisses on your sled,
then barks at us
in winter gear
braving the cold.
I have no time to shoot it,
or the owner unknown for that matter,
your mother's heart –
shattered shrapnel –
like the vase that lies
on the kitchen floor un-waxed
with flowers that cannot mend.

Time is thieving from her soul
like a marauder taking
un-ripened fruit from the tree
yet to grow.
Time you take away in giving.
Tears steam the window.
The humidifier is too efficient.
You and I wave,
you smiling because she is waving
like a robot
without batteries in reserve,
her eyes ready to pop into orbit
in search of a better universe.

You and I must forget her.
Snow will cover our tracks
like a bleached tablecloth
soon to be stained by tires
and yet unspoken curses.

Waxwings sit on branches
like pears pecking at the waning sun
for warmth and frozen seeds.
Spring won't be here for months.
Then the thaw, hopefully.
You and I meet no one on this well-traveled road tonight.
It is cold and cloudless, but we must return
to the woman who calls herself your mother
and is and always will be.
We need insulation in the bathroom,
she greets us with.
Her secret pain ripening as a cherry within,
she plans no supper tonight.

# *The lonely monkey*

Monkeys scurry,
playing human,
the boob tube a ball
then bananas –
reward for correct choices.
You finish your elephant puzzle,
reach within the screen
to belong in the cage,
your new friends beckoning.
You grab at your breast –
your reward for being,
you think,
as others wait like winter ghosts
to stretch the thoughts
I have inserted into slots
to mimic to be yourself,
hoping for reruns of myself
when I am dead.

A solitary monkey,
eyes bulging blindly,
tiny legs quivering,
fingers for comfort at the mouth,
kowtows into a corner of the cage
away from those it knows
not of its kind
in spite of the mirrors that tell it different.
You drop your mother's breast
and wobble up to the screen,
climb into the corner
and hug the lonely monkey,
ignoring the barrier of space
and tube that's supposed to make you an addict.

# The tyrant

The dragon smokes in your soul,
demanding the cow, not just the milk,
to tear off its legs, udder and head
to see how things can be made invisible.
With a mile-long smile
you discard the plastic carcass
onto a mound of animal parts
sacrificed without a prayer.
You then make mincemeat of cardboard folks
retired to farm to beat the recession
you don't yet understand.
Their sudden death at your hands
is somewhat merciful.
They would have starved on the toxic land anyway,
and besides there are more people where they came from.
Humans aren't on the endangered species list.
So you claw at my face,
a mask you think should come off
since it's Halloween.
The skin is mine, however, and sticks in place.
So you grunt words specifically yours,
injected with dissatisfactosyllables,
but you forge forward!
Dolls, whose legs and arms you tore off,
must be resurrected
to regain your attention
so that you can tear them down again.
And so on...
until you've figured out the puzzle
that will confuse you when you do the same
with your life to find meaning.

But for now you gloat,
robbing the squirrel of its hard-earned cones
and defying gravity in your every move,
my eyes watching for smoke to come from your cave
to teach you humility
before your subjects.

# Halloween night

The swans have left
on the frozen lake
images of summers
that may not come,
and it is that time of year again
when we are reminded of ghosts,
goblins, witches and saints
knocking at our door
for sacrifices for a trick
even though we have no neighbors,
or pumpkin lit like a severed head
on the snow.
Yet out here no man is an island,
and viruses do creep in
through the cracks of our cabin
in spite of the extra insulation.

You're running a hundred and four
and climbing
like a comet burning up,
your tiny body so much like the fledgling
without feathers
fallen out of its nest this summer
when you and I nestled it on its branch
where it waited for its first flight.
Your mother's mask of fear
wants to take you in,
while I still believe in saints to come,
the saints of my childhood
who will drive ghosts and witches back
underground where they belong

until next year.
Your smile reminds me of me,
your eyes heavy
and understanding what my father
must have seen before his deathbed,
what I fear for not seeing.
You seem willing to hatch out
into that netherworld
without hesitation
into the frozen lake.
I will not let it happen.
Prayers must still work
in these words that cannot be beautified.

Perhaps the day will come
when I can look into the lake
and see the swan
I once killed for Christmas dinner.
Smiling, I shall be ready
as you seem now,
to fly like a cygnet
on wings as white as light
and embrace It
as I would my mother
who too beckons in the distance
of this night.

# *The onion*

You've eaten the bitter onion
from our garden
to ward off the blues
of years to come.
It will again sprout
in your belly
and shoot out to your very soul
and hopefully settle in your heart.
Its taste will teach you compassion
and that true love shouldn't be given on a whim.

You've also eaten smoked salmon
and you did swim among the streams
only to learn
that salmons die an early death
after giving birth.
You do not envy the fish
and do not care to become one
even if you eat them
with a voracious appetite.
Bananas and oranges you hate
for being sedentary
even though you love trees
and would never cut one down
unless there were a reason.

No, it is the bitter onion
that you prefer.
You have already tasted
its fruit of pain
and the joy of tears.
You have swallowed laughter
like a desperate victim

afraid it might be taken from you.
You are reaching for another slice,
but your mother warns me
that too much of a good thing
can cause depression
and Dostoyevskianism –
an incurable disease of the soul.

Have a praline instead.
It will neutralize whatever damage has been done,
but you greet my gesture
with tears for the bitter onion that you prefer.

# *Mole*

Your mother and I slip
from night into night
days congealed in dreams
of winter that make us blind
as moles crawling through
emotional tunnels,
in search of exits.
You sometimes bump into us,
straying our way
for a collision of feelings,
our eyes needing new lenses
to see your dove-like hands,
still untainted by the sun,
flying about the rooms,
blessing every object,
giving them all souls
with the baptismal of names,
ignorant yet that your mumbling
of syllables is killing
the cat, dog, doll...
with every joyous cry of knowledge.
Perhaps that is why we have yet
to give you a name
or baptize your body in His name.
Perhaps there is eternal life
in just being.

# *The shell*

Your nose stung by the bee
growing in a buttercup,
thinking you a thief
when all you wanted
was to hear its buzzing
up close,
you ran within our walls
like a snail
withdrawing from the pain
that comes from what we think
sweet nectar.
You pointed to the window,
blaming the outside world
like a person condemned.
Your tears abated
and soon the memory was numb,
the image of your nose and bee
erased
and you were ready
to stick your head out of our shell.

# *Another path*

My daughter tumbleweeds in new boots,
breathing the nectar of summer spent
like the tiger swallow tail
she learned to kill with syllables,
my ears attuned to the spelling of trees
felled in the crisp of Fall,
my eyes leashed to her flesh,
her feet faster than safety in reverse.
Another path with roots...
her tracks made and undone.
She falls into the mud, to my happiness,
crying out my name with tears
of pain I hold tightly against my chest
as she grasps a yellow leaf
to sustain the shedding of unwanted skin
to erase the child that holds the key
to the woman hidden in the folds of forests.

# *Space voyager*

You waddle,
stars at your fingertips,
an angel on shaky wings,
smearing peanut butter on the stairs
to assure your safe return,
not unlike Tom Thumb.
The threshold conquered,
you tumbleweed against sleep,
gooseberry eyes exploding with tears,
until you've watered carpet and toys.
Finally, your spirit gives up the body,
even if sleep isn't what you crave.

Your nostrils sense the breast
lying undisturbed in its bed.
I guess, it's too early to give up the nipple
for candy or cigarettes.
Hungry or not,
you wake up from nightmares
your mother thinks you've inherited
from her childhood,
and swim into our bed,
legs kicking like a heavyweight
knowing she is the champion here.

Homeless,
I fall into the couch,
like a mortal punished by ancient gods
with powers that reach beyond mythology.
And in the morning you startle me,
your tiny fingers prodding my nostrils

to see if you can stop up my leak
as you demand I move
from this sacred place of yours...

Exiled,
I banish myself to the outhouse
for some shuteye,
hoping it will be years
before you can climb this autumn hill,
but no sooner has the thought flushed from my mind
than I hear your shrill deter the pine-cone-picking squirrel
from his winter preparations.

# In the beginning was the word

We leaf through the seasons
at the speed of light,
your hand wishing to break out
like a chick pecking
to see beyond.
Wisdom tells me
to guide you
slowly
through the snow
to follow the snowshoe hare,
but you slap in disapproval
and flip us into summer
where boredom on the pond
with croaking frogs
is equally strong.

You are wind in motion.
You shove Alice under my nose,
impressed by the watch on the rabbit,
and we both fall together
through an abyss of images
only you can comprehend
where the word
makes only the sense
it wants to
and is what is without us.

# *Transfusion*

A blade of grass,
wilted,
you lie, exhausted,
by the sun.
If only I could pour
a glass of water,
just ordinary water,
and perk your spirit up.
Were it only that easy.

You cry out my name
perhaps because you think
of me as pain
with pain,
the pain you want taken out
like the eyes
of defenseless dolls' heads
you often pluck out.
I cannot perform the miracles
you have with toys.

Your belly is hot
as sand on a Spanish beach.
It is your appendix, I know,
ready to burst
like a small grenade.
I have seen men's insides out
in fields
where melons still grow
somewhere in the South
where Blacks still plow the earth
now theirs
with mules still.

What are they waiting for?

Finally, a concerned mouth
wonders if we are
who we are on paper.
They are ready for you,
but you do not want to go
with the strangers
I have warned you against,
especially with smiling sly strangers
who promise nothing will happen
when I have already told you
of the knife that will slice your skin.
You will dream a while and awaken
as if by magic.

But things aren't so easy.
You will need blood,
and I don't want to lose you
to the plague
just because of some mistake.
They, of course, reassure
with great manners that the chances of
HER GETTING IT are slim.
I should have no worry, they say,
it's just like driving your car.
My guts are boiling over with anger.
I am not a man of euphemisms.
Once you're dead, you're dead,
I tell them.
Of course, they're not in the killing business.
How could I suggest such a thing?

Today is the first time I have given blood.

## My little helper

You've played with dough
and helped make bread
for the elves you think
live in our part
of the woods only
because your father
is a lover of small tales.
You've touched the blood
of the bull moose I killed,
meatballs you helped
your mother spice.
There is no way
you can wonder
you are eating the bull
that might have visited
our garden last summer.
No, it isn't out of revenge
that I might have killed him,
I tell myself.

Today I've killed again –
spruce hens that deserve
no more killing
than any other creature,
except that they are so stupid
staring like sheep
at the barrel of the shotgun.
I must un-feather them,
and you think
it is fun to see feathers
flying about the kitchen
like miniature birds
of your imagination.

You even find the grey-green
intestines I have gutted
as interesting as the tube
of toothpaste you love
to squeeze just to squeeze.
I split the gizzard
full of cranberries
and fine pebbles.
It ate well,
and we'll eat well.
Buttered and spiced
their bodies look delectable
naked.

## *Your mother will be pleased.*

The oven is ready to accept
the sacrifices we make of life.
You too have found its victim,
standing innocently,
as many have stood,
proffering your clown doll
in a pan to bake with the birds.
Did the clown offend you
that you must punish it
this way?
But you cannot speak
or explain why
even if you could talk.

Children murdered in ovens
not so long ago
resurrect themselves
crying out that dolls should live
until they are grandmothers
and that birds must fly
until they fall out of the sky
like flakes of snow.
Awakened by this revelation,
I tell my wife
we're becoming vegetarians
and that even the fish
have a right to a ripe old age.
She goes along with my moods,
but knows I am carnivorous at heart.
It won't be long before I'm eating
steak and sautéed liver with onions again.

# Owners

Dogs around our neighborhood
multiply faster
than those Bible locusts,
enough to feed China
and more,
each pup famished,
each barking in the night
for love denied
out in the cold
leashed to a tree
to be a dog
because it looks like a dog,
each loyal
to masters on vacation from care
each howling for having been
un-aborted,
reminding owners
of their crimes
in spite of the occasional pat on the head,
good dog, good dog.
But deafness is inbred in humans.
You and I have seen dogs
driving cars,
swimming in pools,
in beds, in boats,
in helicopters and in suits.
Go Dog Go! Go Dog Go!
Stop Dog! The light is red!
And so on...
Now you, too, want one of the pups
to play with
because they're so real.
I warn you of the bite,

not to mention the bark
that already frightens you.
A dog isn't a stuffed tiger.
This morning a dog committed
suicide in front of my car
and I wanted to kill the master
and serve him up the dog he owned,
but you didn't blink
or cry
until you touched its fur
and bloodied up your hand
with life.

# *Perhaps you understand more*

Amy's mother sat in our kitchen,
a place where women come to cry
when husbands leave their senses
or when the women want more
than life can offer.
Your own mother guided a glass
in her shaking hand
to her mouth
as if to a babe in need.

Amy's mother swallowed words
none understood but comprehended
and you felt sorry for her tears
because you, too, have known them.
You patted her knee and smiled
and she squeezed your body
until she was purged of the pain
and you cried in her stead.

Amy's mother flew out,
like a helpless sparrow,
surprised by an early morning snow
and stood in the cool air
waiting
the way we waited the next morning
on a fresh cover of snow
that seemed to celebrate the end
of a summer that had claimed its share
of victims to the drought.

We stood together,
a flock in black,
shedding grief with words

as payment to the living,
warding off death with flowers.
They lowered Amy into the ground,
and I cried for you,
no, for myself,
as you held a plastic rose
to keep you quiet.
Then you waved bye-bye at Amy
the way we tell you to,
even when strangers come to visit,
but you shook your head
in disbelief.

Driving back to the kitchen
where we would fill our stomachs
to appease our hearts,
I remembered standing with my brother
and my pale and withered mother
before my father's coffin,
and when he was buried
and the guests had gone off for beer,
you, my brother, said to Mom,
"We'll buy another father."

# *First visit to the dentist*

Strange as this may sound,
our dentist is a gentle man
in spite of his name –
Dr. Payne with a Y.
We make it through the door
because you are used to opening doors,
and doors, so far,
are just doors.
You go straight
for the giant plastic tooth,
decayed by children's buttocks and filthy hands,
and you sit in the cavity
where you flip through a professional magazine
with a stare so stern
that your forehead frowns,
like a philosopher's,
at work
on the theory that teeth are unnecessary
since you still remember
your mouth being unarmed.
And if God had really wanted us to have teeth
would He have created dentures?
And so on.
Logic is on your side.
A nurse smilingly calls
your name,
and your Spock-like ears
shoot up like radar ready to defend you
against the enemy in white.
You and I pass through another door,
so far,
just another door,
into rooms from which you choose

walls with ferns and trees
and a goofy plaster squirrel
sticking through the linoleum floor
to allay your fears
in spite of your age being immortal.
You find comfort in the cocoon
of the forest we ourselves live in
until the dentist shows his teeth,
like a cartoon lion,
and you laugh for a cautious second,
your gooseberry eyes bursting,
your lungs screaming
as if you were being eaten live
by cannibals.
Undeterred, Dr. Payne proceeds
by experience.
You're not his first child patient,
but proof is otherwise
as you bite through his finger,
your mouth a clam
refusing to be examined.
You will not be defiled
by this particular stranger
in spite of his bribes,
reassurances
and the white smock he wears.
We leave,
unwanted,
and we will not return
until your teeth are ready
to make decisions of their own
and until tooth fairies are out of fashion.

# Harvesting

We're digging graves up
among the broccoli and cabbage stems,
searching for the buried corpse
of your once favorite doll
whose soul may have gnawed at yours
that we are digging this way today.
The reasons for her sudden death
are still unknown.
Perhaps her life was up
once the batteries ran down.
God forbid, mine ever do!
Perhaps your friendship came to the end
like thread off a spool,
and you both outgrew the commonness
that leads to the communion of hearts,
now frozen on a plate,
ready for the eating of the past
to make them live again.
Perhaps that is why I dial old numbers,
trying to resurrect
to embrace
as you now do your doll.

# Mimicry

I bring in
another memory for you,
this one frozen
in a box meant for the Christmas
it will not see
because,
unlike my father,
who still hides behind his gravestone,
playing the ghost he lived,
I cannot keep a secret.
Through this box
I open you as I am,
handing you Madeleine from Paris, France,
a doll meant to instill compassion
because of the appendectomy scar
you quickly discover
after stripping her of the blue coat
and making her into a bald soprano.
Your naked belly yields no trace
of the scar you think ought to exist.
So you vanish in search of remedy
that you quickly find,
crayon in hand
and a thick black greasy line
from rib to bellybutton,
smiling at the wound
that brings back
the ringing of church bells
along with death sentences
passed by my brother and me
scarring each other for life
so that we might compare the hurt
in our old age.

Perhaps you'll never know
a single scar.
Later I shall tell you
of all the bad angels
that flew over our house
and how my childhood healed you.

# Baptism

You kick and scream
against all notions of good,
especially the water
meant to cleanse you.
Yet you drown your doll
in my bathwater
like a Baptist minister
saving her soul for Christ
whom you know not.

My father showered daily,
his body streaming with rivers of coal,
washing down his aspirations
of ever becoming an Olympic swimmer
and once gave me a kitten
to drown by the tail
to harden my boyish heart
against the odds.

Perhaps I understand your fear of water.

# *The butterfly*

We should be a thousand years old,
as you finally manage to tear
winter and summer out of existence
along with the butterflies
that cannot compare to the mourning cloak
we saw
and I captured
in the cell of my palms
to let you peek into the beauty
that I handed you
as a victim to appreciate.
I should have expected the outcome
as you tore its wings
like an eager ogress
searching for the secret of flight
and the precious stones that lit its body.
Then you threw its frail stem down,
disillusioned by the fool I must be
for having expected too much of you
too soon,
as you cried for the other butterflies
you wanted me to catch.

# ONOECT'TOSHTOECT'

Adults attempt
to divine your markings,
like Gypsies tea leaves
to give them sacred meaning.
With certainty
they baptize
with the tip of their tongues
(frog, bat, dove, snake).
Impressionists,
clarifying their views
out of focus,
they ignore your head
shaking in denial
of the truth
for their sake
as if God could be given a face
when you know
it is what it is.

## A kiss

She brings me books,
you blocks, kittens and spoons.
I point to the stars,
you dance the samba and rock-n-roll.
She eats roe,
like fine orange pearls from my fingertips,
candy from yours.
I don't have the breast to soothe,
only the songs I've sung into the sunrise.
She gives you kisses.
I beg...
Do I have to earn them?

# *Perfect*

Had you been born to my brother in Jersey,
you would be inhaling secondhand smoke,
cursing like the dog-killing mailman he is
and watching forty-nine channels
of good Old American television
with a mother that would feed you,
not the breast you are so fond of still,
but bags of potato chips for breakfast,
lunch and supper and in between meals
just because the ads have taught her
to consume while she can without thought
of heaven even though she goes to church
on time on Sunday to insure her a space
in case there is some truth to the rumor.

Had you been born to spiritual healers,
there would be no doubt in your belief
because God would accompany you
on your daily walks like a policeman
protecting you from devils in disguise
and He would speak to you in dreams
to reassure you of your individual mind
in spite of the parroting of words.

Instead you were born to us,
as perfect as a rough-edged stone.

# A Christmas day

You were born on His day,
and to avoid future confusion,
a jade plant stands
where a Christmas tree should
to prevent you from taking on
the stigmas of crucifixion
that comes with speaking one's mind,
but there is no swaying you from your goal
as you point to the babe
Christ as yourself,
not you as Him.
After all, it is your birthday,
and you are unwilling to share at this point
with one unknown to you.
We are not Christians
in the true sense;
we do not go to church
and pray for the death
of those different from us;
we are against all wars
unlike many.
We tell you of this baby
who grew to be a gentle man,
but it is your birthday,
not His as you point to your heart
that can only bleed for itself.
So you decapitate the plaster Christ
and smile as Herod might have done,
happy to be celebrating you,
not Him, who is a stranger
in your house.

We tell you of the wrong you've done,
not a sin yet
(what are sins today?),
and I ask you to kiss the little babe
to make Him feel better
(you feel better)
and then re-capitate Christ,
readying Him for Easter.

# To read your mind

I wish I could devour with your eye
the world you must read backwards,
like a Palestinian girl,
to reach the word
without Webster's.
But to enter your maze
would mean to walk through a forest
where syntax bears icons of me
as in a lover's diary I read on the sly
to get sneak previews of myself
to see that I was still perfect
in her eyes until I fell,
as Humpty Dumpty did from his wall,
for skinny dipping in her subconscious
and swimming in uncharted waters.
To read your budding thoughts
would be to know the day of my death,
when secrets are best kept
locked in one's head.
I think I'll delight in the unspoken,
watching me,
were I you.

# *Tears*

You still grunt like a cave-child
pointing at her parents
who have lost the ability
to speak in your language
understood by you only
because you are the last
of a dying tribe
whose tongue could only be learned
in the womb
and you still have ties
with the homeland
and refuse to let go
of your identity
to blend in the melting pot
where all children are equal.

You must have anti-democratic blood
flowing in you.

To make up for lack of tongue
your tears speak a thousand words,
each drop preciously deciphered
to distinguish pain from frustration,
all coming from a common well
but different.
At times I try to ignore them,
thinking to make you strong
so that you might seek yourself
and find that the fruit in the garden
is there for the picking.
But your tears cannot exhaust their source

as I rush to your rescue
to prevent you from drowning
in the love
you might think lacking.

# *Inspiration*

The geese are honking towards greener fields,
leaving me with the rusty cornstalk
to wait for the snow that insulates our thoughts
to sleep to dream,
but you poke with your red boots
the child locked in my heart
shedding your skin and innocence
like a tiny lizard
hurrying to new cool spaces
whispering in my ear images of a childhood
we shared like a meal
as guests at a table for two
speaking in a strange tongue
no human ever used
showing photographs from our minds
warped by their lenses
worn by time and memory
recalling sweeter thoughts,
sweet because we were
in spite or because of the pain.

Do you recall the afternoon
you buried me in books
to signal my early demise
if I didn't wake up to you?

Now you will.

# It's not a boy

Thanks for not having come out a boy,
a son I would have hated
simply because of the odds
against fathers and sons
repeated over the centuries.
Sons have callous hearts,
soft only for the female flesh,
be it mother, lover or wife.
Sons love the self more than daughters do,
and I want to be loved in my old age
with scars, wrinkles and grey hair
by a daughter with a breath as fresh as pine,
a touch of elderberry wine and salmon.
Sons are unloving.
They love war,
and your mother is glad we will not bury one
or have to wheel his maimed body about forgotten rooms,
the flesh she would have given in vain
for those men of principles.
And sons don't call home on Sundays
or holidays, except when they need rent money.
The son I do have waits for my death
to see what will and testament will yield.

I pity the poor boy who will court you, Lauren.
Lucky for him the sign
"Beware of Father"
already hangs on our fence.
But signs are made to be disobeyed
as princes did challenge the dark.

# *Wilderness*

Young men and women will die on TV
in wars few will recall
except on summer reruns
for mothers and wives to weep
for their losses.
But this is not the path we take,
you and I.
We live in the wilderness,
never praying for civilization
because god could be a bat,
or insect or spring bud.

Today we rode on the wings of ravens,
your orangutan hair spinning
in defiance of gravity
through branches stripped of summer secrets
to the amazement of your finger
pointing at an abandoned nest
empty of hornets
whose stings you've already forgotten.

I stand naked in this forest
as innocent as you.

There is one butterfly. . . there, I say,
pointing at its flight on battered wings,
it, too, surprised
that summer can rob of passions.
Your finger bursts the sun,
causing it to bleed along the clouds
just as your mother yells
that my brother has been killed
unaware still of ants, beetles and cicadas.

The following poems were written after Lauren's death. I have added them to *Lauren At Two* because my daughter still speaks to me at least five minutes a day. And when I visit her grave on sunny days, she and I can still debate issues that are relevant to her existence and mine.

.

# Learning to like broccoli

I mixed your ashes and hair with clay,
glazed you as blue as the white polka-dotted lizard
you once tried to eat,
and baked your semblance to no avail.
I do not have the Maker's magic in hand
to let you live again in my new garden.
I looked for traces of you
among the rotting leaves,
now covered with ash
from a restless volcano
people thought too old.
I even sought your face
as I knelt before the holiest
of moose droppings.
What do I know of true reincarnation?

The starters in my window must be as hungry
for the sun you once thought an orange.
I would like to think that you are
the morning seal whose eyes I seek
always above water
because you swam so well.
But did you really like water?

I can't see you as a frog or bird.
Your soul wouldn't take to them.
It's been weeks.
The broccoli is doing well,
as cruciferous-ly as it can.
Fertilizer helps. It didn't you.
I have cast fishnets over my beds
to keep my vegetable friends for myself,
greed a human trait.

But the moose kept sniffing around,
until you came to claim what is
rightfully yours
as a rabbit without her winter coat.
I called you by name,
and your ears perked up.

Are you here to learn the taste
of the broccoli and cabbage
you HATED as a girl?

# Dying to be a virgin

You tore up another "cartoon boy"
and damned what soul he might have sprouted
to hell!
You have again
taken the vow of chastity
even against imaginary lovers
from those dog-eared romances.
Oh, how you now slaughter them
on the screen you once thought magical!
You've added bacteria to their lips and tongues,
"Thou shall not kiss," your newest commandment!
And let's not mention sperm,
which in your expert medical opinion,
is a virus in the making.

The boys you once craved
have metamorphosed into foxes
you cannot trust.
Like a hen in her house
you know they come to steal your eggs
with smiles and lies.
You are certain you can
protect your ova
by making yourself invisible
as you starve
your future children
before they can descend
into your uterus.

## *Erasing Mom*

The mirror is you
writhing blue faced
in a pool of placenta,
gnashing through your own
umbilical cord
to be free of the shell
you called Mother.
You spit her milk out
before you could distinguish
salt from sugar,
eventually biting off
the bitter nipple from its breast.
You were quick to set
a pattern for future reflections,
unaware that forgiveness
is a wound that never scars.
Your pain, unseen, must have grown
as did your legs and arms
as spindly as a spider's
weaving a web of silence
to trap yearnings of love
out of thin air.
Nothing came your way.
So, you drank blood
from your own streams,
blaming the fat ogress
for starving you.
You saw what you wanted to see –
her favorite pork and pasta as poison.
You kept temptation at bay
as you fell in love
with deception itself,
leafing through fairy tales

in search of your own model.
Slowly, you began to slice meat
from the ogress' bones
until she fit your mold
as the dress I gave you
fell from your invisible self,
your mouth smiling
to see Mother made in your own image.
In the final moment, your heart was purged
but silent of its former beat.

# Cremation isn't fairy tale-like or matter for poetry

Where are we now,
you and I who loved to set the world on fire
with echoes of words pregnant with passion?

I got your last message screaming on my screen:
"I hate her for cremating me, Dad!
You've got to do something!"
Being sent to hell to turn to ashes
never occurred to you.
I am certain you will keep this idea alive
on your still extant hotmail account.
Your sentences were frantic
as you reminded me of your lifelong dream
of your body being encased in a glass coffin
for all creatures of the forest to visit.
Of course, you inserted in parentheses
a young handsome prince on a white stallion
who must kiss your lips
to breathe life into you again.
"How can he do that now, Dad?
How can he find my lips among those stupid ashes?
How?"
I am lucky AT&T doesn't reach where you are now.
Your email is laden with jealousy, hatred and vengeance.
How quickly you turned your mother into the evil queen in Snow White!
How long will it be before you find the poisoned apple?
You beg me for a speedy recovery from this "disaster!"
Since you were 90 percent water,
you think I should just add that amount back to your ashes,
stir three times while chanting a magic spell
I should be able to get from some online witch.com.
As usual, I reply that I will do my best, hoping
you will realize that cremation is final

and guaranteed to last forever.
I am certain your spirit will accept
the fate of your body's frailties, as I hope
I will mine when the time comes.

Love, Dad

P.S. Write when you get the chance

# *A one-sided conversation with a stone*

Geology never carved a crater
into the crevasses of your mind.
You were petrified at the mention of Earth Science
for which you earned a solid F,
preferring metaphors in fiction to sedimentary rocks.

I will never know what you thought of stones,
but they, like all beings, have souls,
except that they speak through the silent syllables of time,
and can be more alliterative than any written page.

Yours is as green as our valley bursting with birch in spring.
It came out of the sand like Venus giving birth to herself.
Your ashes will have to learn the taste of this stone,
and in a thousand years, you will be able to kiss yourself,
perhaps as a diamond.

## Our season

We dip into the wells
of our land,
fencing off the glacier
from our summer fields,
holes made
for your small fingers
to blend with the roots
of trees and berry bushes
we must plant
for our season,
roots that will be nurtured
by decaying halibut carcasses
that will bear red juicy raspberries
and not the fish
you think should swim
on future branches
dangling from cloudless skies
because we have brought the sea
to our land.
Slow as snails
we slide down the slopes,
you slower than I,
me getting slower,
my bones as brittle as pretzels,
ready to nurture the salmon berries
where I will grow among the fireweed
fingers reaching for fish
growing wings instead of fins
for the wind to carry off
once the glacier reaches
our humble fence.

# *Advice to Lauren on her travels*

At the fork,
you and I will have to part ways.
I cannot take the road fated for you
alone,
and I don't want to fall victim
to your vampires sucking blood from my silence.
Learn to be a leech onto yourself
to keep your soul intact.
Don't look so scared.
The forest ahead isn't as hungry for children
as it used to be,
but you will have to get lost
to find yourself.
You must learn to fear,
not to fear the howling of wolves,
and sleep on their hallowed ground.
You must envelop yourself in darkness
and seek refuge in your nightmares
because I will not be able
to shield you from the demons
you will have to conquer on your own.

Everything ahead of us
always sounds worse than it is.
I know.
But the weather is never the same.
Be certain, there will be sunny hours.
You will no longer know cold or warmth,
your body will erase all temptations
that thirst and hunger lead to,
and your eyes will finally
SEE
in your absence among all the nameless flowers.

Your soul will dance
on notes from unsung songs.
And remember, Lauren,
I am not too far behind.
I shall find you on the road
you will have prepared for me.

# *There is inside you*

a shattered bell
that will ring
falsely now,
no time will ever
truly
heal.
But within the dome
resides a forest
where paths lead
to where the dogwood grows
and the squirrel waits
with a key in its paw
to soothe your heart
to sleep
so that you can learn
to ring the bell
with your own voice.

# Echo and Narcissus

I sit at a boarded-up station
not expecting the train
that took my childhood
through pastures now empty of cows
to a beach with no sand.
I wait for that old volcano
to blow its hot head
to thaw the grieving ink from my pen.
My inbox has been empty
of illusions for months,
queries rejected before they're ever read.
You once had faith in every word I wrote down.
I miss seeing me in the mirror
as I grope for the face of day.

# Martyrdom? Greed? Hungry for love?

You were starving.
I fed you pieces of my heart.
You were thirsty.
I let you drink from my veins.
You were cold.
I fleeced my skin to keep you warm.
You died anyway.
I have nothing to give you
but memories of scars
from your avid mouth.

# B-----a isn't a word

I smelled the end of summer
at the sight of your bloated belly
before your spring could even begin.
The poster child for a starving Ethiopia
didn't become you.
The pussy willow remained unsung this Easter Sunday
and no tiger swallowtail kissed your fingertips with her feet.
I warned you of winter's long silence
you seemed to want to make
as sacred as your iconic smile.
I told you would NOT make your bed
so that you could dream of resurrection
from some kiss-and-tell fairy tale prince.
Why couldn't you awaken from being unloved?
Why did you want to be invisible to see yourself?
Why do I stand in the absent foot prints
of last summer's quarrels?
Are the seal's eyes yours come to peer into the sorrow
I cannot yet forgive you for?

# *Accepting*

You have hundreds of eyes screwed into that head of yours!
Some are the usual fare: auburn, brown, blue, and green.
You do, however, prefer azure, iris, vermillion,
and even café latte.
But the set you really want is purple with clouds that move
from eye to eye.
Still, you haven't made up your mind, which pair would suit
your sockets best.
"And why should I just have TWO eyes, Dad? Don't you know
how blinding that is? I want to see the whole world at once,
not just slices of it!"
You've loved chameleons for as long as I can remember
and suggest contact lenses.
That you say would be dishonest,
especially when every being's spirit resides in their eyes.
I leave it all up to you
in spite of those two-eyed humans staring at your head.
Earthlings will just have to get used to you
or grow more sets of eyes.
It's that simple, I say.
"That would be cool, Dad. Real cool!"

# The Flowering of Lauren (1989–2009)

The gardener's seed grew in a solitary spot
he watered and weeded.
A trunk emerged with branches out of season,
but no matter how much he prayed, the sun
never seemed to warm his tree.
He breathed on the plant to give it life,
and because he loved his tree with all his heart,
it gave him flowers of various shapes and colors.
People were amazed and told the gardener
how beautiful his creation was,
but the kind praises didn't deter blight
from taking root.
The tree lived for several seasons,
losing its blooms and leaves.
Then its branches and trunk rotted from within.
The gardener's heart was frantic to find a cure,
but none of the potions he tried
could revive his beloved tree.
When the people heard his creation had died,
they gathered at the gardener's orchard
to know if the news was real.
When they saw nothing grew where once beauty
bloomed, they wept so much from love
that their tears awoke the spirit of the tree
as it grew back before their eyes.
The gardener rejoiced as he gave them cuttings
to make sure his tree would never die.
He asked them to call it the Lauren Tree.

6449586R0

Made in the USA
Charleston, SC
26 October 2010